FARM ANIMAL STORIES
THE PIG

Kingfisher Books, Grisewood & Dempsey Ltd,
Elsley House, 24–30 Great Titchfield Street,
London W1P 7AD

First published in 1989 by Kingfisher Books

BRITISH LIBRARY CATALOGUING IN PUBLICATION DATA
Royston, Angela
    The pig.
    1. Livestock: Pigs – For children
    I. Title   II. Series
    636.4
ISBN 0 86272 442 2

With thanks to Mrs A P Cloke of Manor Farm,
Chadwick Lane, Knowle, Solihull, W. Midlands
Series adviser: Dr Bryan Howard, University of Sheffield
Edited by Jacqui Bailey and Veronica Pennycook
Designed by Ben White
Cover design by David Jefferis
Phototypeset by Southern Positives and Negatives (SPAN),
Lingfield, Surrey
Printed in Spain

FARM ANIMAL STORIES
THE PIG

By Angela Royston
Illustrated by Jim Channel

Kingfisher Books

It is a hot day in summer and the young pig longs to be cool. She is very thirsty. When she sees the farmer filling up the water trough she trots quickly over. As she drinks, the water splashes her feet.

Then she wallows in the cool mud bath she has made. Other pigs are drinking too. One of them digs a shallow trench and lies in it, feeling the cool earth around her.

Evening comes and the young pig wanders over the field searching for food. She roots in the ground with her snout and finds a fat worm. Then she eats some dandelions and tufts of grass. She even eats some of the earth.

She flops down in one of the huts and falls asleep. But almost at once an angry snort wakes her. An older, stronger pig wants to sleep in this hut. The young pig leaves quickly and has to find somewhere else to go.

Summer passes and the young pig is nearly fully grown. One autumn day she is rooting near the fence when she sees a gap. She pushes up the fence with her snout and squeezes under it into the wood.

She wanders a long way through the big wood, feeding on chestnuts, acorns and mushrooms. At night she finds a dry ditch. She is tired and settles down in it to sleep.

The farmer wants the pig back. Early the next day he finds her and uses a wooden board to guide her into his truck. Then comes a bumpy ride back to the farm. The young sow would love to explore the wood again, but the fence has been mended.

The sow is seven months old now and she is ready to
have her first litter of piglets. She is put in a sty with
a large boar. The huge animal grunts and nuzzles
her sides. The sow grunts back and stands very still.
Soon they mate.

The days get colder. The pig shares a hut with another young sow. They make a nest in the straw and huddle together to keep warm. One morning they find the field has turned white with snow.

The pigs do not mind the snow and take huge bites of it. It turns to water in their mouths. They hear a tractor coming into the field and trot towards it. The farmer is bringing them food, water and straw.

Spring comes at last. It is nearly four months since the pig mated with the boar. All this time piglets have been growing inside her and her belly has been getting bigger and bigger. Now it is nearly time for the piglets to be born. She is taken to a farrowing pen and given plenty of fresh straw. Using her snout and trotters she builds a deep nest.

The first piglet is born early one morning. The small wet animal struggles to his feet and searches round his mother until he finds a teat. One by one the other piglets are born and soon all ten of them are noisily sucking milk from their mother.

The piglets grow quickly. They play in the straw and climb all over their mother. Each piglet always suckles from the same teat. The piglets who have the teats nearest to the mother's head grow fastest and biggest because they get the most milk.

One day, when the piglets are three weeks old, one of the larger piglets pushes her way through the door of the pen and into the farmyard. All the rest follow her. They find lots of exciting smells here. They chase the hens and root in the mud.

But they soon get very hungry and rush back to
their mother. The farmer has just filled her trough
with food. Their mother slurps and gulps down the
food while the piglets, squealing with delight,
clamber over each other to see what is going on.
They eat a bit of it and find it tastes quite good.

The piglets are given more and more food and soon they are feeding from the sow only at night. When they are eight weeks old they no longer need her milk and they are put into a separate sty.

Their mother is taken back to the field. She digs her snout into the green grass, happy to smell the fresh earth again. She has already mated and will have another litter of piglets in the autumn.

More About Pigs

The pig in this story is a Chester White. It is farmed outdoors. Landrace pigs are usually farmed indoors. The Poland China is a popular pig in the United States and the Gloucester Old Spot is a popular outdoor pig in Britain. Tamworths are very hardy outdoor pigs, common in Australia and Asia.

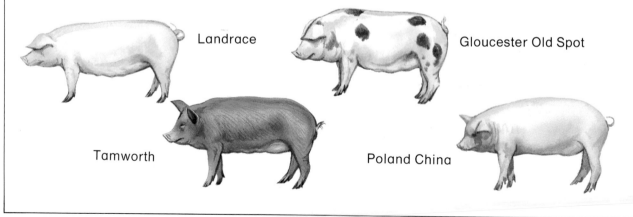

Landrace

Gloucester Old Spot

Tamworth

Poland China

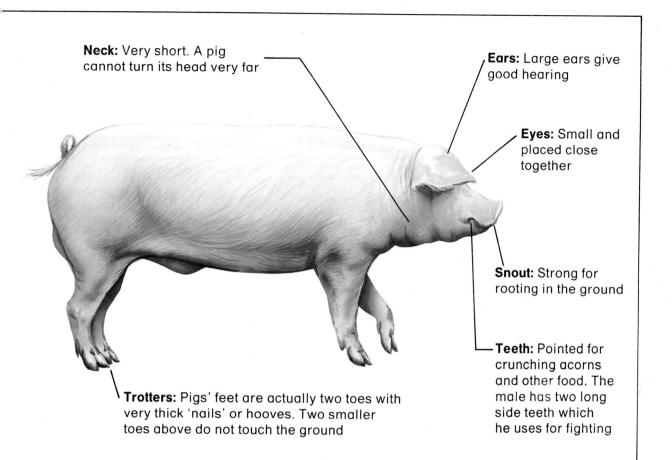

Neck: Very short. A pig cannot turn its head very far

Ears: Large ears give good hearing

Eyes: Small and placed close together

Snout: Strong for rooting in the ground

Teeth: Pointed for crunching acorns and other food. The male has two long side teeth which he uses for fighting

Trotters: Pigs' feet are actually two toes with very thick 'nails' or hooves. Two smaller toes above do not touch the ground

Pigs are clever animals and have a very good sense of smell. In France they are used to find truffles, an expensive mushroom-like food which grows under the ground. Pigs can sniff out the truffles and dig them up, but they have to be stopped from eating them as they are a pig's favourite food!

Some Special Words

Boar A male pig.

Farrowing Giving birth. A farrowing pen is a special pen where the mother pig can give birth to her piglets. It protects them from foxes and often has a heat lamp to keep the newborn piglets warm.

Litter A group of piglets born together. Pigs usually give birth to ten or twelve piglets.

Rooting Pigs find their food by pushing their snouts into the ground and turning over the mud.

Sow A female pig.

Sty A pen that pigs are kept in.

Wild boar A wild pig that farm pigs were bred from. Wild boars are still found in parts of Europe, Asia and Northern Africa.